Philosophical Poetry:

Crowns & Shattered Dreams

BLACK AUSAR

Copyright © 2020 by Jason L. Shankle

All rights reserved. This book may not be used or reproduced in any manner whatsoever, transmitted in any form or by any means – electronic, mechanical, photocopying, recording, including information storage and retrieval systems – without written permission from the author, except in the case of brief quotations embodied in critical articles or reviews.

Published and Edited by Jason L. Shankle

AUTHOR

Black Ausar has been writing poetry since the age of 10. His pen served as a way to comfort himself during the dark moments in childhood and adolescences which transcended into philosophical poetry entries. As a creative writer it became his therapeutic medicine to express emotions he couldn't voice. The layout of his compilations of poems brings you along an unforgettable warrior walk through the streets, dreams, and love... The heart of who he is now and evolution of himself lives in every word. He currently resides in Denver, Colorado.

Social Media Outlets:
Facebook, Instagram, Tik Tok & YouTube:
@Book.King.Publishing

Books available on website:
www.bkingpublishing.com

Dedicated

To the God in me

HOW THE STORY GOES

CROWNS

My Soul Journey | 15
Story About Bread | 17
Must We Dig Deep to the Soul | 18
Thankful | 19
Glory | 20
Nothings Forever | 21
I'm Trying | 23
Life is a Crazy Ride | 24
Knowledge | 25
Long Story… | 26
First Rhyme | 28
Vulnerable | 29
NOW | 30

MINDSET

Connections A Weapon | 32
Why??? | 34
The Subject | 36
Deep. | 37
Isolation | 38
Reasons | 39
ight | 41
Teaching to Learn | 42
ART | 43
Random Introspection | 44
I Can | 45
Fear What? | 46

BLACK

Know Thy Self | 48
Unapologetic Knowledge | 50
Wake Up. | 51
Am I A Hostage | 54
(Spell) ing (Words) | 56
Black King, Black Man | 58

STREETS

My Name is Money | 60
Drugs | 62
Influence Over Change | 63
They Want to Hear More | 64
Momma Use to Say | 65
Steal $1 Lose $100 | 66
Cold Bowl of Soup | 67
Survive The Real | 68
Unappreciated | 70
Wasted Talent | 71
W.W.M.D. (What Would Music Do?) | 73

SHATTERED

Pain Taught Me Everything | 76
What Childhood? | 78
Smoke The Pain Away | 79
The Past | 80
Fakelationships | 81
Some of Us | 83
Last Impressions | 85
Insurance | 86
Live, Life | 87
I Let Me Down | 88
Never Done | 89
I Should Charge Me | 91
Loaded Questions | 93
Deep Thought | 94
Black Girl Lost | 95
Walked Away | 96
I Don't Want to be Famous | 97
It's Never Enough | 98

HEART

Love, Love | 100
Queen Questions | 101
Twin Flame | 102
I Understand You | 103
Twice | 104
Amnesia | 105
Narcissist | 106
Vibes | 108
Crystal Clear | 109
I Don't Trust You | 111
Mathematics | 112
Cheating with Jane | 113
Mental Stimulation | 114
Make Up to Break Up | 115
Reciprocity | 116
Jezebel | 117
Un-In-Love | 119
What is Love? | 120
You | 121
Walking With a Goddess | 123

DREAMS

Compared to Love (Dedicated to my Momma) | 126
I'm Dreaming
(Dedicated to Martin Luther King, Jr.) | 127
Very Necessary (Dedicated to Malcom X) | 129
Yo, Fred! (Dedicated to Fred Hampton) | 130
THUG LIFE (Dedicated to Tupac Shakur) | 131
Prolific (Dedicated to Nipsey Hussle) | 133
Kicking Philosophy
(Dedicated to Mario Flowers) | 134
A Story To Tell (Dedicated to Nas) | 136
Old Voicemails | 137
Rest in Peace Old Me | 138
Father, Son, Holy Spirit
(Dedicated to my late-Father) | 139

LEGACY

To My Son | 141
To My Daughter | 142
Together | 143
Legacy | 144
Why I Breathe | 145
God | 147
While I'm Alive | 149
Bless My Tribe | 150

CROWNS

My Soul Journey

Long time coming,
Never running from my problems,
Too many issues,
And Word Up magazines,
I felt grown,
Barely knew my kin,
I don't have friends,
Only childhood brothers,
Loyalty cheated with betrayal,
So, I kept faith,
While stretching rubber bands,
Hardly watched TV,
I refuse to be cultivated and/or vaccinated,
History is a trip worth taking,
Hate, I hate you,
Until I realized real lies,
Feeling your pain like an Empath,
Being satisfied with things,
I'll never be,
Bless this ugly beautiful story,
I'm lead director,
Editing the script,
Manipulation versus world news,
Now, I can channel my energy,
I've finally forgiven me,

Yahweh guide my soul,
Show me where to go…

Story About Bread

Bread will get some people killed,
Talking that real spill,
In the Most High I Trust,
I shall be still,
There's loafs to feed everybody,
At least the illusion of it,
Bartering my spiritual appetite,
Back against the wallet,
Living on borrowed time,
Broken promissory notes,
Can't loan out my heart,
Finance finesse,
Never impressed with dough,
I will rise.

Must We Dig Deep to the Soul

This must be how Nas felt,
In the booth making Ether,
CRAZY
We knew it was coming,
After Malcom's last speech,
UNIQUE
The richest person in history,
Is an African King named Mansa Musa,
TRUTH
Young tragedies remind of Fred Hampton,
PEOPLE
Tell a lie loud enough they will…
LISTEN.

Thankful

I just need you to remember,
What I taught you,
Keep your word with your "self",
Fast forward the past,
Echo chamber mind control,
Know over exaggeration,
Haters can't make my agenda,
I'm booked,
God gave me a second life,
Under water baptized,
The old me died,
To be alive,
Despite all the evil attacks,
I'm happy,
My enemy's hell is inside them,
Yahweh's purging people out my circle,
There's some funerals I won't be at,
So, I can arrive at this higher Chi,
Thank you for everything.

Glory

Glory is earned,
I wake up at sunrise,
With my back pains and mental stress,
But still you never forget,
It seems like I don't do enough,
For the things you do for me!
I pray every night,
Honestly,
I see and realize,
I'm worth it,
Glory has no due date,
Survive the deadlines,
It's already done,
I'm at a point in my life,
Where I'm tired of saying,
How come?
My past has passed away,
I finally have glory.

Nothings Forever

Even if I trip,
I'm going to fall where,
I am supposed to be,
Going back like I left my keys,
Prayed so hard broke my rosary,
Do us both a favor,
Don't get close to me,
I might snap,
Say something I can't reverse,
Stop caring about "becauses",
I felt agape love,
Complete my soul,
Devil knocked on the door,
I wasn't there,
Stared at death,
There is no fear,
When you live under Ra,
The suns first name,
Religion destroyed everything,
This is my opinion,
You don't have to believe it,
Why you judging?
This ain't free,
She was my reflection,

So, I married me,
Bottom of the ocean deep.
Forever died,
Never cried,
The beginning looks similar to the end,
God's DNA is in my skin,
You can call us twins,
Even if we die together,
Nothings Forever.

I'm Trying

Watched my momma struggle over bills,
Getting gray hairs,
Know we won't stay here long,
Daddy never called,
I got the message,
No fatherly direction,
Pray I don't get lost,
My intuition raised me,
Let's go this way,
Be calm,
It's just the dark,
I can't feel my heart,
Too much pain,
Kept my head up,
Like I'm drawing the sky,
Heard it a thousand times,
I believed it once,
Second guess the experience,
I don't do everything for love,
It's kind of a gimmick,
Playing the game,
To try to understand,
Who I am?

Life is a Crazy Ride

Lately I've been arriving early,
Getting to my destination in a hurry,
I'm not feeling my feelings,
After this big bag,
Self-made without the artificial,
Mental minimalist,
Grandiose dreams,
What the hell does that mean,
I never fit in any category,
Landed on the wrong planet,
Shouldn't of took that left turn,
Damn it.

Knowledge

Without the "**K**",
Leaves "**NOW**",
And if you can't take an "**L**",
Pushing me to the "**EDGE**",
K-N-O-W-L-E-D-G-E

Long Story…

Pushed all my chips in risking to win,
Just keep your word,
I don't need no new friends,
This world's a long trip,
You got a lot of nerve,
Searching for love,
Destiny's so sure,
Her favorite artist Tupac Shakur,
I figured that,
Black is the same black,
I read for truth,
Watching Hidden Colors,
Everyone's imitating us,
It's no longer flattery,
It's humiliating,
Death to the opposition,
Compassionate listening mixed with blatancy,
The devil can wait,
Had a deep convo,
To describe the system,
In one word I'd say "cage",
I'm raising Kings and Queens,
Your hustle must be real,
Can't eat ideals,

Cowards will never answer the questions,
Thank God I broke up with Jezebel,
Hard heart and cold,
As a prison cell,
Attempt to make me suffer,
What an epic fail,
Time traveling,
To find out…

First Rhyme

I stack my 10's and my 20's,
Even dimes and nickels,
And when I started using game,
It was fundamentals,
Now I'm a pro,
I'm not a buster,
I'm a Negro,
That likes lots of money,
In my pocket,
Or my billfold.

Vulnerable

Trying not to cuss,
It's hard to trust,
Fluck,
Quick right turn,
Will I arrive?
Am I alive?
Mind full of locked rooms,
Food for thoughts on the dinner table,
Social constructs started with concepts,
This makes intimacy impossible,
I don't leave voicemails,
Hope I don't fall back,
I'm just praying,
Body language "guarded",
More-Heart-Less

NOW.

There is nothing more important than now.

The past is a ghost.

That only can breathe with your energy.

Now is more pivotal than the future.

Because you have to be alive now,

To see it,

What is more important than?

NOW.

MINDSET

Connections A Weapon

I'm so sure,
I must keep cool,
Life will give you jewels,
That look like rocks,
Safety off,
Energy exchange,
I don't have change,
It's the same thing,
Whatever you cash out,
You'll get back,
Who you think you are?
This has went too far,
Have you disarmed,
I bear the truth,
Loves a dangerous game,
Full of bullshit and bliss,
Cupid shot an arrow,
I hope it miss,
Aw shit - I'm hit,
Doing things,
I never do,
Loaded up on artillery talking to you,
Extended conversation clip,
Mental stimulation shocks the brain,
Keeping my peace clean,
I could have died,

I'm appreciative for every night,
Grateful of the mornings,
By the Most High,
Always connected.

Why???

You are who you think you are?
I am, I am,
While society tells me,
You will be….
At the same time,
Doesn't know me,
I find it hard to answer questions about me,
Although I am climbing to a higher height,
Talk about internal irony,
As an Erudite,
I am the master of my fate,
But if you don't have the funds,
There will be blockades,
No matter how long you point out hate,
Or the weight of your GPA,
I can only access through enrollment,
In a system designed to do,
Exactly what it is doing,
This is not complaining,
But proclaiming the truth,
Forcing deep thought,
Indifferent situations,
I'm the underdog,

Influenced by this burning passion,
Setback, mishaps and struggle,
Keeps this fire alive,
Navigating this puzzle,
To know the end is far,
Had to use my foresight,
Educational street mentality,
When am I not teaching,
Is the evaluation,
First generation to break the curse,
Minor examples,
Still, no answered questions.

The Subject

Prejudice teacher,
Can't get out her implicit bias,
Mindset is idiotic,
Employed because you went to college,
Shaking my head,
What a damn shame,
Nothing changes but the same day,
Hiring identical principals,
There's no principles,
The system is a spider web,
Not hard to understand this,
You can't have selective ignorance,
Turn the light on for enlightenment,
Reject the brainwash,
I taught myself to think.

Deep.

The light bearing upon,
Which we live,
Hoping to bring,
Form to ideas,
We pursue illumination,
Giving name to those ideals,
Until they are nameless and formless,
Felt experiences,
Dreams birth concepts,
As understanding,
Living those fears,
Losing their control over us,
Dark with hidden,
Ancient places,
Holding creativity and power,
Of emotions and feelings,
It is deep.

Isolation

Past interactions with others,
Shaping personalities,
Choice, experiences and relationships,
Including difficulty expressing emotions,
Identify and explore feelings,
To empathize while practicing new ways,
To foster connections,
Or isolate?

Reasons

Make even these odds,
Don't want to hear,
Anything at all,
Another voicemail received,
Salting your food,
Before you taste,
Probably what you're doing,
When you're assuming,
We don't like each other,
Crazy motha..,
Watch your mouth,
Whip me down,
Too grown to play around,
I can read,
Seen the signs,
My life is mine,
I thank you for bad times,
Sarcastically okay,
Yeah, nah?
Any way,
I'm the best,
Lames dying for fame,

Cleanse my mental space,
Decisions sleeping with questions,
You'll never know my reasons...

ight

I don't have all night,
My spirit embraced the fight,
Kept my iron tight,
Protect my families light,
Lose my mind I might,
You don't feel my Plight,
Yahweh bless my Sight.

Teaching to Learn

Knowledge is illusive,
Unless you ask sharp questions,
To find something,
But is purposeless,
If you don't want much,
You have to spread your wings to fly,
Better than your arms folded in a casket,
As an adolescent,
I was hardheaded,
Deep down in my heart,
I'm always ready,
I already knew the cost,
So, when I am learning,
I can teach you,
While I'm still learning my "self" …

ART

Can't spell heart,
Without art,
It would only leave he,
I'm not scared of the dark,
Follow the light,
Risk my life for expression,
Writing while driving,
God take the wheel,
Known dying legends,
The thing I hate the most,
Is that we'll no longer hear their words,
Break out this programmed jail,
Quiet loud silent messages,
Staring at this perfect imperfection,
Creating what I see.

Random Introspection

Don't be a box on my checklist,
Had to draft a Will,
No one's stronger than death,
Don't ask for a loan,
If we aint getting along,
I'm the first to say,
I'm dead wrong,
Aiming to live right,
Only if I had one night,
Some ugly truths make us lie,
You know what's up,
Keep in mind these lines,
Can't hold nothing like a fake pocket,
Artistic energy is everything to me.

I Can

Even when I was timid,
I wouldn't be scared,
Father wasn't there,
Secret language is "figure it out",
Didn't get to be a kid,
I thank my mom for all she did,
Still remember my first stanzas,
Get it done with urgency,
Do before it's due,
Basketball was my way out the hood,
Strong chess moves,
Pop talked about respect,
Momma taught through strife,
Cousins was Thuggin',
As a youngster,
Developed a palette for hungry,
Fell in Eros-love with my hustle,
Crazy relationship with trust,
Foresight is a must,
Never ever say
"I can't"
You can,
And if you believe,
You will!

Fear What?

I remember I cried when Pac died,
And I know I will when Nas does,
Drove me to a conclusion,
Power's an illusion,
That's probably why I love the Blues,
And the saxophone in Jazz songs,
Pain is so soothing,
If I had to choose an addiction,
It would be healing,
I no longer think about trauma,
Too many miles away from drama,
Me?
I will have an enlightening night,
Frame things I can't control,
Placing it in its proper place,
So, I won't drown in an optional race,
I simply don't know how to be fake,
This poetry entry right here,
Sounds just like Proverbs,
And if you're not committed,
Don't pretend you lived it,
The cost is expensive,
Nothing more desired than freedom,
Fear What?

BLACK

Know Thy Self

Father-Son-Mother-Daughter,
The world shot at my Holy Spirit,
Out of body experience,
I featured myself,
Sage on my dresser,
Wisdom on the shelf,

Cut from the Kings cloth,
No fabrications,
God is the same black,

I hate when you late,
Wrong turns and stereotypes,
It's a fact we civilized everybody,
Ready for war like St. Maurice,

If you not prepared,
I can see why you scared,
Stole the ritual from spiritual,
I remember,
Packaged manufactured religion,
Mass production of fear,
Which is why people are zombies,
No need to assassinate you,
When you're conditioned,
You'll do it yourself,
Protect me ancestors,

From these evil culture vultures,
It's called acculturation,
They want our rhythm,
But don't want our blues,
In the name of who?
I've already burnt Santos wood,
I know thy self,
Do you know thy self?

Unapologetic Knowledge

Living in a land poisoned,
With western cultivation,
Some of you may be thinking,
What does that mean?
I'll explain everything,
Because we are the beginning,
Before all races and creeds,
And it sure wasn't,
The Europeans or Greeks,
Comparably 1492 is new,
Mother nature is uncouth,
History pages are glued,
Pharaoh's look just like me,
Melanin potent and rich as cocaine,
First identified as an intelligence gene,
I pray wisdom overlooks lady truth…

WAKE UP.

I am rooted in my Blackness,
I know actually who I am,
Stop thinking you only come from slaves,
Yes, always pay homage with no currency,
But understand when the White man,
Believed the world wasn't flat,
They followed an African made map,
Straight B-line for Black,
From Kush to the U.S.,
Far before their presence,

So why doesn't the history books mention that?
Africans brought Christopher Columbus,
To this undiscovered promise land?
Notice how it is downplayed,
By false heroic stories of mass murders,
Numerous Sand Creek massacres,
Blood could feel the Nile,
And denial on behalf of many,
White supremacy beneficiaries,
I come from the true Kings and Queens,

That trace back to Pharaohs in Kemet,
While White history tends to be so romanticized,
Which is why you must analyze,
The praise of religion,

Depictions of bleached paintings,
And HELL NO!
You can't have my Black soul,
The media has demonized,
Beautiful mahogany,
The more I search my spirit the moor,

My Tribe,
Must be protected with compassionate love,
And understanding,
The first statue of liberty was a Black woman,
Breaking shackles of slavery,
And arrogantly replaced with a White woman,
Leaving the chains still attached to each ankle,
From the original design,
Symbolic Black Queen,
And when I use more it is M-O-O-R,

This enriched Blackness along endless accounts,
Of dark-skinned Emperors and Rulers,
As confident as I can sound look it up,
Knowledge is much like melanin the deeper,
Europeans and other races dig in history,
The beginning of civilization leads to Blackness,
We are entitled with the historical privilege,
To greet each other as Kings and Queens,
Know your descendants,
And if others had the diligence,

To explore one's heritages beyond dogma,
Will realize you would not exist,
If it wasn't for me and our melanin skin,
The letter "C" in America,
Was used in order to help you not see,
Nor read the Willie Lynch letter,
There is no duality in body and mind,
How bold,
To change names and accounts,
Like the 16th century "J",

Changing the name of Yahweh,
For English purposes,
My God what could have happened next,
Are past steps,
Dismantle the slave mindset,
This universe is the classroom,
WAKE UP.

R.I.P. To all our injustice Black youth, men, and women from the beginning of time.

Am I A Hostage?

People meet me,
Then say,
Whatever comes to their mind?
I am no longer concerned,
And this fast I'm on,
Has my neuro racing,
Damn I'm indecisive,
Well I messed that up,
While my false self replies,
What?
Mental handcuffs from my control,
Trying to take me back,
Are you happy?
Well yeah,
Naw, but really though?
This is not a dilemma,
Avoid this future crash,
I'm under pressure,
I won't stay depressed,
I'd rather go "through it" then "Let it go",
The old me could of have died,
While eyes open,
With an empty AK clip,
Bob Marley blunt clinging to my lip,
Waiting to give Aaliyah a kiss,
Is this misery?

King Solomon was labeled one of the wisest,
But couldn't figure out,
How to have one wife,
Everyone has bottomless wants,
The truth is too honest,
It's so relieving,
No regrets is how I will live,
So, this strife is just me in the moment,
Trauma in my psyche,
Paid the ransom with pain,
My decision is what it is,
Because I'm alive and made it pass 25,
Seeking faith through divination,
Did I ask the right questions?
I will never be the same,
It is a gorgeous struggle,
Knowing that nothing matters,
Self-love should be effortless,
Crossing the bridge,
To heaven for an eternity,
Inside of me…

(Spell)ing (Words)

Let's pray,
What do you praise?
Title without the ing,
Be careful of beliefs,
If these walls could talk,
I wonder what the ground would say?
I'm from the streets,
I can't speak,
English is a curse language,
That's why we cuss,
I know just enough,
It will not suffice,
Can't write what you can't read,
They lied about the tree of life,
Strange fruit,
Son - Sun,
Are you confused yet?
Wear - Where,
I'm already,
Their - There,
Purposeful mistakes,
Protect your top,
So, you don't get brainwashed,
Eye - I,
Most use one,
Orishas kill the fear,

Here-hear
Listen up
Books lie and people die,
Opinions aren't facts,
GOD-DOG
Even got us reading backwards,
It's your fault,
In whatever you believe,
And you wonder why,
They are called,
Spelling **words**.

Black King, Black Man

No one has our plight,
Devils in hell want power,
You don't know the pressure,
Of a Black King,
Searching for your Queen,
The opposition don't want you breath,
Or have anything,
Write and tell the perfect lies,
Fabricated why's,
Listen thrice for whatever you heard,
Black man learn your true story,
Because you're the first original King.

STREETS

My Name is Money

I'm the dirtiest thing,
You can put in your mouth,
Because everyone's hands been on it,
People's DNA's stained on me,
You need me,
Bet not cheat me,
I can buy anything,
Make a shy person sing and rap,
Everybody's working for me,
Don't go out the front door without me,
They say life ain't free,
We don't know who "they" are,
I feel like a brand-new car,
Near death by far,
I change the meaning of barter,
While paying tithe's not in the Bible,
I'm an expensive opinion,
Costly decision,
Dollars make people listen,
Leave some missing,
Cold-blooded motives,
And life insurance policies,
Strip clubs call me rain,

I give you a place to stay,
Enemies lie on me everyday,
I will make a way,
I know I stress you,
Chasing me will exhaust you,
Even neglect your children,
Hustlers finesse for me,
In God We Trust,
Is tatted on my chest,
My favorite color's gang green,
You find me,
You'll found your heart,
So, I never sleep,
No period,
Only commas,,,,,

Drugs

The world will never be enough,
Every street code,
Especially in corporate,
Dope for the hopeless,
Fame is an addictive substance,
It's a bottomless pit,
You want more and more,
Can't tell when your full,
Every generation thinks drugs is cool.

Influence Over Change

Trust said you don't have faith,
Rejection said get out my face,
Plead the 5th I don't know shit,
Sometimes I go nuts,
Over my cashews,
Barley had new shoes,
Dysfunctional relationships,
Taught me about lust,
Ignorance broke my crutch,
Complicated loyalty to love,
She wants it in present,
And she tastes,
Like a Now or Later,
I studied her,
She's major,
Drama was minor,
Fractioned my mindset,
Then met my twin flame,
She healed my solar plexus,
Belief creates everything,
I choose influence.

They Want to Hear More

That meant a lot to me,
When he got off the stage,
After pulling an Andre 3000,
I saw the search,
Thought they were confused like church,
We need our flaws,
He didn't listen to the applause,
"They want to hear more",
But you gotta stop,
Reading off your phone,
We were quiet because of the shock,
Rehearse in the mirror,
So, you can see it clearer,
If you don't get it right,
It's an artistic mistake,
I have this look on my face,
Because "we want to hear more".

Momma Used to Say

Don't be a brilliant mind,
Behind closed bars,
You only get one chance at life,
And if you survive death,
Means you're blessed,
The streets ain't your friend,
Did you wash your hands?
Respect makes a man,
Always do your best,
Be thankful for every breath.

Steal $1 Lose $100

I'm working on my mental settlement,
They couldn't prove their evidence,
Even the devil said he was heaven sent,
Either you pay or you pay,
Misery will take everything of value,
That's why you broke for nothing?
Counted blessings after a Bankrupt spirit,
Justice's weighed with a scale,
While blindfolded,
In God We Trust,
On all money,
Make belief,
Most took it,
Literally.

Cold Bowl of Soup

Over $20.00 dollars,
You jeopardize this relationship,
Better yet forfeit,
We're not going forward,
I will always love you,
This is where you get out,
Even if you don't know,
What I'm talking about,
You can still grow,
Just not in my garden,
Unconditional acceptance of no regrets,
Non-Negotiable on disrespect,
What makes it more sad,
Is that you don't see it,
My actions make you believe,
Soul messing up your sensory,
Your vibe fell off from the frequency,
Temporary pleasure,
Void of stress but blessed,
As far as this decision,
I must transcend.

Survive the Real

Thirsty in the morning,
Hungry at noon,
By the time night comes,
I'm ready to make moves,
Value menu, chips and tap water,
This diet isn't cutting it,
Can't remember the last time,
I had a three-course meal,
Not only tired from how it is.

But sick from how it feels,
Power of the dollar bill,
Help you survive or get you killed,
Fill out an application get hired,
They ain't trying to pay,
Because the color of your face,
Society wonders why we distribute drugs,
The devils put it here,
How'd you think it got here?

For sure wasn't grown here,
During the 90's we didn't know,
Anyone in Columbia or Afghanistan,
A known secret,
For how long?
It's time to sing a new song,

To make money,
In this uncivilized structure,
That wants us to die.

It's oblivious,
Despite being the most gifted,
They consider exceptions,
But in the hood,
Easy to buy weapons,
Not complaining,
Because there are no fair wars,
Rest assure when underestimated,
The score will be even.

Whenever you cheat,
It shortens your breathing supply,
Choking off air to your brain,
Already knew I was insane,
Holding me down,
So, I can't breathe,
Assisting in trying to drown me,
Above the ground,
Until the last day,
When there is nothing to eat,
We will see who survives.

Unappreciated

Pain, I paid that,
Receipts bring rain,
I'm used to getting counted out,
You owe me now,
High off self-esteem,
I'm coming down,
Mind in my thoughts,
About things that irritate me,
I haven't completed,
You needed to hear this,
Concentrate on my energy wave,
You're never alone,
We need our wrongs,
Unforgiveness is normal,
Just don't let it become you,
Silence is wise,
When you're not wrapped too tight,
God saved my life,
Yah, it's in your hands,
Direct this pen,
Footprints meeting my feet,
While carrying me through the sand,
Unappreciated.

Wasted Talent

My man!
52' inch vertical no lie,
Wanted to be a dope guy,
He took it literally,
45 points, 9 rebounds, 10 assists,
45 clip, 9 Milli, with 10 packs,
You had a good game bruh!
Such a perfectionist,
Thinking about that 1 rebound you missed,
Posted up by the light pole,
Running cardio around street corners,
Scored a triple-double anyway,
Bags full of money and muscle,
Made it to practice every morning,
High School phenom,
Got the city ablaze in two ways,
Highlights on ESPN,
You'll hear his name,
#1 basketball player in the state,
2nd in the nation,
Only because they were hating,
His winning percentage was better,
Held every record in the district,
However, kept the full court press,
With it off safety,
Mind stays ready like a loaded gun,

Threw his shoulder out,
From moving duffle bags,
The brains a canon,
What a .38 special,
You can feel the soul,
Big momma used to say, "Let it go",
It's in the Lord's hands now,
Don't let it grow,
Consoled by the ancestors,
Heal it don't fix it,
I think I emotionally abused forgiveness,
Only street disciples,
Can understand this narrative,
You know how this story ends,
Prison or Death,
To be continued…

W.W.M.D. (What Would Music Do)

This beat is so deep,
I can't sleep,
Embracing the energy,
If I was sound,
I'd be your favorite song...

You influence my spirit,
Bass on my ears,
Speaking to me in my darkest moments,
So many genres,
I can go on and on...

Hip-hop understands me,
R&B taught me love,
Didn't see it much in my household,
Marching to my own drum,
Melody keeps me calm...

The 70's was so soulful,
Less commercial,
More acoustic,
Goosebumps when I hear classics,
There's a message in the lyrics...

It's the feelings of healing,
No instruments,
Navigating this noisy world a cappella,
Don't know where I'd be,
Music saved me.

SHATTERED

Pain Taught Me Everything

Growing up I lack support,
Like a broken chain,
My Carlos Rossi jar,
Full of pocket change,
No male influence,
Beside my older brothers,
Out all my mother's sons,
"I gave her the most trouble",
In and out of court,
As if it was a sport,

Then I looked myself,
In the eyes,
And said,
"I'd never cry",
I had to box my ego,
To check my pride,
Life's a gamble,
You must make it worth it,
And when I transcend this earth,
My children gone hurt,

I can't decide which one's worse,
Leaving whys or conclusions behind?
Even the devil's kind,
The Most High is in my veins,

I have a gut feeling,
I won't lose,
Refuse to be weak,
Having dreams of the streets,
Trying to kill me,
Envious of rest,

Damn, I can't sleep,
I'll stay woke!
The descent of this roller coaster,
Gets me depressed not anxious,
False love is a misused discharge,
It's not negative if you're real,
And when I spoke into the mic,
I meant every word,
My journeys been turbulent,
I want to soar,

Stop wanting more,
Land on stability,
With both feet,
The blind man told the wise man,
We must wait to see,
Because your pain,
Can't live without your heart,
It is essential to understand,
This trauma root,
In order to heal.

What Childhood?

"I won't say it twice",
You must be a man,
There's no time to cry,
Why waste why's?
Even the wise,
Experience foolish moments,
No one's exempt,
It's not that simple,
Kind of like learning a bike,
Catch on when you fall,
Numb and detached,
I hope I find you…

Smoke the Pain Away

A shower from a rainy day,
Where the hell is my lighter?
Can't even lie to you,
The gorgeous ugly truth,
Now what am I going to do,
After the news,
I couldn't move,
Repress it because it's too much,
Never believed in luck,
Strange people stuff,
Crazy things I do for love,
Being traumatized was normalized,
Just like that my life changed,
Strong in my veins,
Hard to get through it,
I don't give a damn if you judge me,
I have the right to remain high,
No choice but to be numb,
It hugs my lungs,
Stops the bleeding,
Light enlightenment,
Make it thru the week,
Defer my thoughts about it,
Than take a deep inhale.

The Past

Living in the past,
Never assisted me to score,
Visitor on my home district court,
How do you know you are healing right?
When it hurts,
Bliss is worse,
So ignorant,
I was selfish,
Now I think I'm too selfless,
Fell in love with now,
Past tense.

Fakelationships

I made a lot of mistakes,
But I ain't fake,
Hard not to sin,
When you're obsessed with winning,
In this oppressive systematic structure,
It's a game of Russian roulette,
They want to Trump us,
Going to the top,
Slightly paranoid but hyper focused,
I'm not fearful of heights,
You're a fish on my hook,
Still Soul Searching,
Like my first book,
Even if I was standing on an earthquake,
I wouldn't be shook,
Can't learn to swim,
From an instruction manual,
Get grip of your handle,
The past you must let go,
If it comes back then you know,
Blindsided for the third time,
That's what we get for Romanizing,
Parable lines,

And if everyone knows this,
Couldn't it be manipulated?
People can be so damn phony,
Never ever say it to your face type stuff,
Jealous of luck,
Probably hate Yah,
No loyalty.

Some of Us

Some of us have Words,
Some of us have Guns,
Some of us have Funds,
Some of us have Blunts,
Some of us have Connections,
Some of us have Pens,
Some of us have Paper,
Some of us have Knowledge,
Some of us have Pain,
Some of us have Faith,
Some of us have Loyalty,
Some of us have Pride,
Some of us have Lessons,
Some of us have Regrets,
Some of us have Passion,
Some of us have Hustle,
Some of us have Losses,
Some of us have Costs,
Some of us have Friends,
Some of us have Moms,
Some of us have Dads,
Some of us have Family,
Some of us have Sadness,

Some of us have Streets,

Some of us have Money,
Some of us have Prophecy,
Some of us have Angels,
Some of us have Orishas,
Some of us have Protection,
Some of us have Weapons,
Some of us have Queens,
Some of us have Kings,
Some of us have Enlightenment,
Some of us have Life,
Some of us have Crowns,
Some of us have Third Eyes,
Some of us have Tears,
Some of us have Years,
Some of us have Darkness,
Some of us have Light,
Some of us have Kids,
Some of us have Legacy,
Some of us have Now,
Some of us have You,
Some of us have Me,
Some of us have Us.

Last Impressions

The experiences of life,
Waking up in the a.m.,
With my mind missing,
Asking stress where is it?
Usually where it stays,
But cheated with worry,
Used to live on early death street,
Root veins running all over the map,
High blood pressure next to hypertension,
What my momma say,
If I don't listen,
Hard to eat with no food,
In the kitchen,
Easiest thing next to sleep is roll a sweet,
Your assumptions about my cover,
Will make you miss a good book,
Learn to judge a person the second time,
Instead of when we first meet,
Last impressions.

Insurance

You're at fault,
This is going to cost,
Whoever has a witness gone win,
Hell of a game,
You don't even know my name,
Your assumptions are reckless,
Sign this contract,
Just in case ish happens,
No capping,
What an evil plan,
"Let's make money off death",
And if people don't fall in line,
Bury them alive in debt.

Live, Life

Why blame me?
Why do you care if I'm crazy?
There's still father-less babies,
The average man appears to be lazy,
Look forward to what?
No answered phone calls,
Strategize my position,
I'm not comfortable,
I know how it goes,
It ain't meant to be told,
I will play my role best way I can,
I'm only a man,
I live right now,
Anything can happen,
No longer desiring the answers,
Y?
X out every task,
Go to the end like the letter Z,
Been living a tough life,
Is something wrong?
You can tell me,
Dirty money schemes,
No good people would do anything,
You must survive,
And risk your life,
To live.

I Let Me Down

You can move around,
Or I can direct you,
No more trauma loops,
What goes up must find the ground,
Hard to believe people,
Keep my experiences to myself,
Aim at riches to conquer wealth,
But you're nothing without your health,
Stop analyzing others and blame yourself,
Waiting on time,
You let you down,
Damn, I can't fix it?
This is going to be painful,
I let me down…

Never Done

Never done until the King of Kings arrive,
You live in the middle before,
You make it to the end,
Just know who's not your friend,
Try my best to stay out the way,
From areas not for me,
And be at places I need to be,
Overcome all obstacles,
Breaking hundreds,
Would never change me,
Won't let my heart burden me,
Is something I don't care to see,
I've been down so many times,
It's beyond me,
I forgot to count,
Can't eat if you don't have bank,
Chasing money marathon,
Not willing to wait,
No matter where you're from,
It's about where you're going?
The tops really lonely,
The opposed so fraud,
Keeping my head right,
Laces remain tight,
The battles only begun,
Anticipating the 12,

I won't dwell,
I knew it was going to come,
I am never done,
The King…
One

I Should Charge Me

Reminiscing about pain,
I don't know why,
I put myself through these things,
Feeling the wind against my skin,
It's hot outside,
That's why I love the shade,
No longer bothered by people,
Talk behind my back if you want,
My therapy is truth,
I can finally see the beautiful day,
Misery's strange...,
Every merciful moment,
I'll always pray for atonement,
There's no such thing as normal,
Instead I welcome problems,
Disappointing broken promises,
I should charge me for this notice,
Ego sit back for the ride,
Intrinsic intuition,
I've had a lot of people die,
Energetically, I'm never alone,
I admit that I'm numb,
Life as a Black man,
What a phenomenon,

Few relationships made my spirit sick,
Avoiding now as I visit the past,
Thank God I'm more loving,
Get lost in my favorite park,
I found my heart.

Loaded Questions

First question?
This will blow your mind?
Do I hate time?
I wonder what God would say?
How do I co-exist?
In a world like this?
Where the hell's the exit?
Can I believe this?
Yes-Maybe-No?
How'd I survive my mistakes?
Where are my ancestors?
I have another question?
House or Home?
Left-Wrong-Right?
You want to pray tonight?

Deep Thought

Laying on some bread,
Like a Po Boy,
Grew up around poor folk,
Turn down the noise,
Smoking loud,
Alone in crowds,
I wish I really could relate,
Can't take a joke,
Hard to be happy,
How'd I get like this?
All I can do is sit and think.

Black Girl Lost

Background club music,
Said it was murder,
And you can't wait,
To rush to the bar,
Getting stupid drunk,
But when we talk about,
The Higher God within,
While time disappears,
Don't want to visit your homeland?
Searching for Amen,
Beauty is her curse,
Get it in your dome,
Bitterness on the lips,
Another liquor shot,
She gone lose her keys,
Can't find that $20,
Ending every night,
With "Where's my license?"
What a symbolism...,
Identity?
Name: Black Girl Lost.

Walk Away

There are times when it's okay,
To Walk Away,
Leave it on the table,
I Walked Away,
Fear said I was scared,
I Walked Away,
I didn't care when,
I Walked Away,
Death yelled for me,
I Walked Away,
I tried to understand before,
I Walked Away,
To my disloyal friends,
I Walked Away,
We can never be together
I Walked Away,
**The light is near,
Don't Walk Away.**

I Don't Want to be Famous

When you have money,
You always have friends,
Hang out with you because your car,
Since age 10,
"I swore I was going to win",
Took my anger out on the world,
I was tired of sleeping on the floor,
My childhood is looking for me,
Mental age grew faster than my peers,
Becoming a man,
Remember the first thing,
I had to grieve it out,
Good advice is very wise,
I'm thankful for our energy transference,
Heavy dialogue about fame and love,
Spiritually soulful,
I will remain humble,
Famous for what…

It's Never Enough

I see money in the future,
You can say I'm prophecy,
After profit before a lot of needs,
I stand by the truth,
I won't take no pleas,
Enemies can't get my soul,
Trying steal my shine,
Keep negativity out,
Seeds die and then you grow,
Don't know what you don't know,
What you think?
Falling hoping I land,
Both feet in the mud,
Ancestors protect my footprints,
I refused to be brainwashed,
Paid everything plus cost,
I'm my own boss,
It's a dirty game,
You'll never be satisfied,
I want more.

HEART

Love, Love

You ain't fall in love,
You fell for love,
No difference love,
Love to love,
Reluctant love,
Pain lust for love,
You sexy love,
Hate to love,
Light healed me love,
Thought it would kill me love,
Living my dream love,
I'm so happy love,
Passionate love,
Heartbeat love,
Forgiving love,
We can do better love,
I need love,
Understanding love,
"I'm patient love",
"I have a question love?",
Let's pray love,
We'll find the answer love,
Our spirits knew it love,
Love, Love...

Queen Questions

Mentioned the question twice,
I said yes,
Yes!
OMW,
I didn't even leave yet,
Sweat dripping from great responses,
Fantasize of you on top of me,
It started with an important question,
Poured out honest confessions,
You have a body shaped like the answer,
I need to do it every time,
Ask me anything,
Good lawd,
She was raised in the library,
Forever mentally stimulated,
I know you have a question,
My Queen,
Let's hear it,
I'm compassionately listening,
Taking a mature walk through each other's past,
Plus, she loves to laugh,
I can't wait to taste honey.

Twin Flame

One of a kind,
It was numerous evenings,
I thought of someone like you,
I felt 20 years ago,
Something was up,
Maybe in our past lives,
We'll remember,
The difference is in us,
This wasn't lust,
Or living in the false self,
My spirit introduced me to you,
Your questions kept me grounded,
The formula helped me grow,
It's an experience,
Just hearing your voice,
Healing my brain,
No matter what we go through,
It's about what we're building,
Finally got a good card shuffle,
No more gambling,
I knew it was you.

I Understand You

This is soul searching poetry,
On my mind like a brain scan,
Don't work for me,
We'll partner up,
Want to have that type of love,
Where you can speak your spirit,
Say anything,
And I mean ANYTHING!
Take the moment inside when you break,
Counting our blessings,
We are 1,
Not 11,

Don't bring those 00's around,
Let's keep it 100,
I'm seeing 1's on every clock,
Hard to quit,
You're my cigarette,
I won't let you forget,

A full body tour,
Found what I'm looking for,
No longer lost,
Understanding is loves real name.

Twice

Only want to get married once,
Never choose to divorce,
Minds a bedroom,
Seductive blackout curtains,
Great night is making love twice,
Healing our past wounds,
Debate and then laugh,
We gone make it through,
It's going to pay off,
Started my life twice,
God you were right,
I'm on an odyssey,
Obliviously,
Prophet after profit seeds,
Gail spirits produce rotten soil,
I lost everything then made it back twice,
So, we can relax to mellow music,
Pray over my family,
Blind man said, "Wait and see"
Whatever you are seeking,
Will find you,
You can't die twice…

Amnesia

This is a wrestling match,
I lose,
You win,
A seductive yes!
Lick on your curves,
This interaction gave me,
Amnesia about my ex.

Narcissist

I'm out of fuel,
Making it through the dark,
While you gaslight me,

This is a direct question,
Put down those verbal weapons,
Even if they won the lotto,

They wouldn't be happy,
You just want control,
Are you going crazy?

Stealing narcissistic supply,
Straight face lie,
Void of all logic,

Simply because you said it,
It's only about winning,
And cheat to crush you,

Children are pawns,
Living for the drama,
The most terrible actors and actresses,

You will ever meet,
Tried to trap my soul,
Who the hell was I with?

Never protect your enemies,
If you know,
You know.

Vibes

Why you looking at me like that?
If you didn't want me,
To say something,
I know the difference between,
Attraction and passion,
I get what you are putting down,
I don't need captions,
We have an R&B frequency,
Send me another song.

Crystal Clear

She would say,
"I'm living my best life",
When she was younger,
Want to be a wife,
But who is she now,
She has no clue,
Taught her daughter nothing,
Poker face lookin,
I pulled her card,
Telling the truth?
I know you bluffing,
Stupid joker,
Pretending to have money,
On the gram,
She gonna flex,
Choosing drunk weirdos,
Perfect reflection of misery,
It's a mess,
Put that on God,
In Jesus name,
Her mother worse,
"Grew up in church",
Earned her Gail spirit,
Father named Ahab,

Produced a rotten apple,
Sure, we go way back,
It's been sad,
"I don't give a damn if he's a good dad",
Blot on your legacy,
Sucker MC memories,
Ripped off the universe,
You have to pay it,
Missing purposeful receipts,
You'll never get my energy,
Broke heart chakra,
Gave away her soul,
She'll die miserable,
Period.

I Don't Trust You

Sometimes I want to say forget you,
Hate to see what your love does to me,
And I feel like your too critical,
Self-talk reporting bad news,
I'm about to take another risk,
Lusting over the same stuff,
Looking at my reflection?

I Don't Trust You

Mathematics

I really don't want to be,
At odds at all,
I'm here 2,
Add two you,
Not subtract from u,
Never want to be,
Divided,
Use this formula to heal it,
With multiple O's,
One day we can multiply,
Break out of these (Parenthesis),
Can't let life overwhelm us,
We'll get our numbers right,
Lay on my balance sheet,
Wire me your love,
Standing next to you,
We make an equal sign,
Return On Investment,
I double checked,
Calculations are correct,
I did the math.

Cheating with Jane

I smoke grandiose weed,
Because I do big things,
How bright is your light?
I'm quite blunt,
I couldn't marry my wants,
She moves with allure,
I spend time on you,
Because you accept me,
You help me think creative,
Relieve stress and pressure,
Long distance from drama,
Baby,
You massage my calm,
Relaxed not numb,
Only when you leave,
My lady hates you sometimes,
But you stay respectful,
Making love on the balcony,
Then lay next to my wife.

Mental Stimulation

Intellectual conversation,
We get dumb lit,
Laugh over funny shit,
Utilize social media outlet messengers,
May the Most High manage us,
Take care of our gears,
When we in the clutch,
More like debates,
Never a monologue,
Intimate dialogues,
I won't say arguments,
I can hear your mind,
When you're not talking,
Not vicariously,
I want to love your spirit,
Speak on your darkest feelings,
I desire understanding,
I'm listening,
I have questions....

Make Up to Break Up

Every morning she gets up,
She puts her face on,
To cover up flaws,
I can't see at all,
But we know they are there,
Make up to float through the moments,
Wants what she wants,
Don't get in her way,
Better be in route,
If you on your way,
Five languages of love,
Scored the highest on,
Words of Affirmation,
Studying your body,
Focused on the exam,
While she's testing your eyes,
Something about that look,
Stare is so loud,
Are you lying?
Do you really care?
Getting home broken down,
Wiping off her makeup,
To put it on the next day.

Reciprocity

I want you so bad,
You already know that,
Freeze for the Kodak,
We can paint time,
With this mind frame,
To touch without touching you,
What we have nots lust,
Both loud we can't sneak,
Pleasure until I won't speak,
Recycling our energy.

Jezebel

Now, it's real Jezebel,
Oh yes, I love her like Egyptian,
Hieroglyphic encryption she's never honest,
And bought me a soul-tie for my birthday,
Learn the enemies' name,
Because they'll study you,
She'll fuck your brains out so you can't think,
Next thing you know you become an Ahab king,
Passive as a flame dodging the rain,
Numbers lie if you ask her age,
Capricorn ram so she climbs mountains,
Despising the fountain of repentance,
No need to apologize she's not listening,
Cut your tongue out then ask questions,
Now, **it's real** Jezebel,
Resentment killed her smile,
But still got her body though,
Beauty is her hearse,
Pretending to have a family is what she cloned,
Sold her birth right for a bowl of nasty soup,
Just to not be alone,
Even though she grown,
With both parents in the home,
Ask her about positions she knows plenty,
But a place with God she doesn't know any,
There's no self-love,

In love with lust,
Rinse in misery and repeat,
Now, it's real **Jezebel**.

Un-In-Love

You made me **Realize**,
What wasn't **Reality**,
Hate should **Never**,
Look like **Love**,
Even if you're mad at **Me**.

What Is Love?

You inspire me to discover things,
I couldn't see,
On my own,
The fact you've grown,
In my destiny,
Sometimes I wish for perfection,
Will you fade without pain?
Would you know the differences?
Is Love really Love?
Was I in Love?
Or ever loved?
Forever, Love.

You

Up all-night writing,
I couldn't fight it,
Irony of a healer,
Take down your pillars,
Paint a horribly beautiful picture,
Grieving over the old you,
Mirror, Are you still true?
Destiny kissed me,
It tastes good,
Spirit in full pursuit,
Falling out the galaxy,
Hoping I land on my soul,
Everything we don't know is waiting,
For a bad excuse,
Or explanation,
Love at first sight,
Deserves a second look,
Reading this closed book,
I'm a vibes person,
Love must trust respect,
To water growth,
Raising our family,
Most High peace,
Reject lower frequencies,
What a wonderful melody,

Polish your seventh chakra,
Protect our castle,
No place we can't go,
Literally and figurative,
You're the only one I sing for,
Imagine all things I would do to you,
If you let me,
From a long distance her eyes invited me,
Where are we going now?
Itinerary read destination "support",
I've never had this,
One thing for sure,
Nothing's definite,
Even with evidence,
Knew you in middle school,
"Yeah, J you smooth",
I don't do these things,
You made me break all my rules,
It's you.

Walking with a Goddess

Put it all on the table,
Like we gambling,
Everything's a risk,
Always a juicy kiss,
Staring deep in your eyes,
While your aura feels the room,
Anticipating the future,
New role coming soon!
You're beautiful star,
She asked me about my heart,
Sexy demisexual,
You don't know it,
Look it up,
It turns her on,
I ran out of words,
I gave her my dictionary,
That's hilarious,
Even when she laughs,
It's my favorite sound,
I pledge to keep you smiling,
Heal generational curses,
Crack the Emotion-Code,
I feel your soul,

I already know,
Either tears or raindrops,
Will water our seeds,
We chose both,

You're what I need,
I unconditionally accept you,
Familiar same spirit,
My sole-mate
Walk with me babe.

DREAMS

(Dedicated to my Momma)
Compared to Love

The value of money to love,
Equals nothing,
A single mother raising,
Four boys on her own,
Can be compared to nothing,
Through all this evil,
You grab me every time,
Refusing to let the devil in,
And out loud announcing,
I am the golden child,
And these are my children,
Whatever I have they have,
Which is what God has given me,
Compared to love,
Which is more powerful,
Than anything.

(Dedicated to Dr. Martin Luther King Jr.)
I'm Dreaming

Running a race full of pain,
Two wrongs don't make a right,
It'd probably make a circle?
I am a dreamer not a drug dealer,
Even though both require hard work,
Having faith in yourself,
Is putting God first,
It's called a race because it's a race,
No one will win,
I don't believe the propaganda,
Taking this test for an "A",
But if I was letters,
I wouldn't be OK,
Martin was right about our great souls,
We made it through the darkness,
For light to illuminate,
In war there's no such thing as Shutdowns,
I know what I don't know,
Rest a sure I will chase knowledge,
Dr. King would have been proud,
Happy and sad at the same time,
Truth is truth,
You don't have to eat the fruit,
Go back to the beginning,

When color couldn't kill hope,
And know who we are,
What a dream…

(Dedicated to Malcom X)
Very Necessary

What a famous line,
Love when I hear it every time,
Passionate Taurus,
Thunderous sound,
Didn't even need a mic,
We have rights to bear arms,
Enough is enough,
I'm not eating,
Or drinking the poison,
Kill whatever that noise is,
They fear speech,
And terrified of truth,
Wasn't a Pastor,
But Malcom could preach,
Voice was so unique,
Progress requires discipline,
The more they'll sell you,
Addictions to growth,
The mind is a business,
If he was still alive,
We would have peace,
By any means.

(Dedicated to Fred Hampton)
Yo, Fred!

We are the people,
This world is evil,
He came back like a sequel,
Press the pen to your temple,
Started with a shot through the peep hole,
Freedom was dying to live,
We can't shade the truth,
The universe is on our side,
When he held a townhall,
He made Black and White people relate,
They thought it was scary,
Then he was targeted,
Named him the Messiah in the files,
Watch Fred's old speeches,
Humanizing intellectual lessons,
The first to shout the message,
Power to the people.

(Dedicated to Tupac Shakur)
THUG LIFE

He still lives on September 13th, 1996,
A legend is gone,
But still here in essence,
Listen to the records to learn lessons,
Reconciliation with staged elections,
Bullets pierced the skin,
Five times,
Your mind is the ultimate weapon,
Struggle, understanding and sacrifice,
Keep ya head up!

It's gone be alright,
Never lose your demeanor,
This is the fight of America,
Covering things at night,
Sentence a man to life,
For minding his own business,
The enemy hit the switch,
To kill the lights to the show,
But little did they know,
They resurrected his soul,

Resembling hustler's hope,
Gold represents paper,
I'm not hungry!

Even when I say it with humor,
It doesn't sound funny,
They don't give a fuck about us,
Now that true money.
To Tupac the Muhammad Ali of Hip Hop,
Putting you on game,
Before his tick-tock stop,

Never watch to watch,
Concrete street corners,
In the ghetto projects,
Martin Luther King, Blvd.,
By any means necessary,
Malcom X speaking,
Outspoken Fred Hampton,
Make it clear like James Baldwin,
They all enrolled in Heaven,
With their souls graduated,

On the behalf of what?
Who do you believe in?
Enlightenment word drive-byes,
You can't strike me,
The enemy wants to dictate,
Even evil fears,
We must destroy tyranny,
For our unity,
Rest up young king.

(Dedicated to Nipsey Hussle)
Prolific

Hustle Young King,
Hustle,
Feels like I lost a family member,
Cold as Denver blizzards,
Hotter than Park Hills Summer of Violence,
I will always remember,
To run the race,
Pass the baton,
Nip would say,
Diversify your net worth,
For your legacy,
To have all money in,
Revise and define,
Weight on my shoulders is a ton,
Living life to the end,
Your sacrifices tell you,
How old you are,
Your behaviors snitch on your actions,
And how much you know,
Determines your pace,
In this marathon called the fast life…

(Dedicated to Mario Flowers)
Kicking Philosophy

You were one my best friends,
Young dogs that grew up,
We talked all the time,
You never liked to cuss,
What is a curse?
Deep thought talk,
Dissect the jargon in small paragraphs,
At the bottom of all contracts,
We knew,
The Four Agreements,
"Let me borrow some knowledge",
I remember when you,
Put that book under my doormat,
The New Earth before,
I flew to New York,
True story,
To us,
Wisdom's a spirit,
People will believe a lie,
Then praise fear,
Philosophical analysis,
You made a difference as a therapist,
Office was down the hall from mine,

We never got to chop it up,
At City Park,
"You can't do everything for love",
Man, that convo was memorable,
One of the most intelligible,
Large empathetic heart,
Mario helped a lot of people in therapy,
I still see your finalized business plan,
Holding it in your hand,
A Dream House come true,
Rest Easy

(Dedicated to NAS)
A Story to Tell

America,
I want to talk to you,
I gave you power,
Life We Chose,
Last words,
What goes around,
Breathe,
The Slave and The Master,
If I Ruled the World (Imagine that)

Old Voicemails

I got your voicemail,
I would of called you right back,
If I knew it would be the last,
Mario made it look Easy,
Rest In Heaven Little Brother,
Learned so much from each other,
Our Kicking Philosophy sessions,
"Oppression handcuffs growth",
Beat the hell out your destiny,
My purpose keeps testing me,
Perfecting my recipes,
Anxiety comes from society,
Pop, I hope that you're proud of me,
That final voicemail was so funny,
Reminders of you,
You died on Sunday,
I'll always be your son,
J,
Missed out on your grandkids,
God called,
You picked up...

Rest in Peace Old Me

Let them envy,
If anything that's gasoline,
To my destination,
Tall influence,
So, I don't get short changed,
Wasn't always who I am now,
Cold as no love,
Transitioned into a Healer,
My road led to becoming an Empath,
Weak jaws would get stiff jabs,
Can't miss what I never had,
Unforgiveness was my norm,
A young man that loved anger,
Replaced rage with sage,
Life happens in intervals,
To be who I am today,
Was ordained,
Not a miracle,
Brush this dirt off me,
I died to myself,
I'm born again,
Rise. New. Me.

(Dedicated to my late-father Matthew Shankle)
Father, Son, Holy Spirit

I am a spitting image of you,
Most of what I stand for,
My moral character was instilled,

With love and joy,
Respect, Loyalty and Family,
Wise words spoken,

If you knew,
Or met him once,
He would of influenced you,

Champion spirit for God,
And he still lives on,
One of my past best friends,

I can't wait to hug and laugh again,
Love you, Pop.
Rest In Peace

LEGACY

To My Son

I believe in you, son,
I know you don't know,
Much about my childhood,
That makes two of us,
Didn't want you to grow up like me,
T.V. in the closet,
Hope I don't get hit with a stray bullet,
I Thought drive-byes were normal,
Ain't gonna lie,
I was probably traumatized,
Not writing this to be glorified,
Gods on the inside,
Young Black King,
I will never give up on you,
At your age I was learning about guns,
I'd rather teach you how to read,
I knew you would figure it out,
You can walk in understanding,
And run with knowledge,
Present in the universe's classroom,
Better yet know your purpose,
You been worth it,
Move in wisdom,
Because no one has the plight of a Black man.

To My Daughter

Intelligent young Black Queen,
Your gender is the birth of civilization,
Know that your beauty is not a curse,
You speak and look just like me,
This world crazy baby,
Never believe your less than a man,
Matter fact your melanin,
Makes you extraordinary,
Love your SELF with compassion,
Remember my teachings,
Be a bright light,
Don't let media prescribe,
False perfections,
Never restrict your mind,
While we all have beautiful flaws,
Your presence taught me love,
And relationships don't complete us,
Tap into the Goddess in you,
While God lives through you,
Simply because you are you!

(Dedicated to Jason, Jr. & Jael)
Together

I'd die for you,
Even kill for you,
Never lie to you,
Only to protect,
And don't do the what if's,
I hope you remember,
All I taught you,
Including every time we laugh,
It hurts to sacrifice,
Love highlight the way,
I'm thankful for every day,
Y'all mind is just like mine,
Question the universe,
While we stared at the stars that night,
Affirmed my children will be alright,
You are me,
Even when I leave,
You know I'm still with you,
Always,
Signed: Together.

Legacy

No one lives forever,
I'm going to share this while I'm here,
The birth of my children were my best years,
Y'all make it worth it,
Every grind,
Valuable sleepless nights,
For my children,
I'll put my life on the line,
Sacrifices are never meaningless,
Can't forget the hard times,
My purpose is to teach understanding,
Mold your mind,
Heal your own heart,
Pass my knowledge down,
Enlighten your crown,
Family.

Why I Breathe

I know when I die,
My children gone miss me,
I want them to know I wasn't scared,

I smiled at death,
Fought until I had nothing left,
Their ear on my chest,

Listening for a heartbeat,
Won't believe the sound,
I know you gonna worry about me,

I'm up in heaven,
Having a shot with Grandpa,
Even though I never met one,

We can hang out in your dreams,
Still go to get ice cream,
I love whatever you sing,

I know this hurt you,
You have strength to make it through,
Protect my legacy,

All my kids just like me,
Junior you know what to say,
Mymy you know what to think,

Never forget God's in you,
Stay grounded in heavy steps,
Climbing the Tree of life,

We will find the root,
That's why I always told you the truth,
I'm in you so I'll never die.

God

You don't hear me,
My past tried to kill my dreams,
Manipulation slept with dogma,
Enlightenment gave me speech,
Reading forbidden books,
My Spirituality fell in love,
At third sight,
Prosecuted by destiny,
I plead "purpose",
Money said it ain't worth it,
Death is the end of the movie,
Not a eulogy,
Late to your own funeral,
Light is dark I know,
Can you hear that?
I don't think you're listening,
Matter of fact I know you're not,
Fiction vicious thoughts,
Father, Son, Holy Spirit,
Where did the Woman go….?
Or the Soul?
Ima leave that there,

I have faith,
Not fear,
People really don't care,
Evil is not a cold you catch,
Or racism a flu you caught,
Nor hate an accidental habit,
You can keep your excuses,
Where did this word God come from?
I would ask that,
There are so many important things,
Every religion has something in common,
Which is why I'm spiritual,
No spirit without ritual,
Put it together,
Searching all over the world,
But in you….

God

While I'm Alive

Tell me you love me now,
On my Nipsey Hussle,
King me on this chessboard,
Dream Team nightmares,
Birds soaring in shattered air,
Protecting this Crown,
Above my Third-Eye,
Truth is sacred,
Had to divorce fear,
Can't help but be passionate,
I'm a Taurus,
Kiss my Astrology,
Studying this calendar,
Spelling out J-A-S-O-N,
Planning without a future,
I was cheating on myself,
I found what I was looking for,
No more Soul Searching,
My hearts made up,
Mindset let's get it,
My twin flame healed me,
Broke my rose quartz,
God is in me,
I forgive you.

Bless My Tribe

I just got out,
I realized my freedom,
When I had no control,
Can't willingly walk-through doors,
Evil lurked in the walls,
Sitting down to be judged,
Top enlightening convo's,
No daylight,
Questions make you close,
Formed a new perspective,
Hope for the greatest story,
Catch my loved ones like an eagle,
I know so much lingo,
Yes, It was painful,
Wild how things give you life,
That was meant to kill you,
No concept of time,
I want my children to be wise,
Staring at the ceiling,
Thinking about living long,
Can't be mad,
I meant every word,
Momma taught me love,
Still don't cry,
On my life,
Bless My Tribe.

Books also by author:

Therapeutic: Soul Searching Poetry
Limited Edition

Sufferless: Meditations for Transforming Trauma
into Healing

From the book:
Sufferless: Meditations for Transforming Trauma into Healing

"A healthy person to me is someone who adapts to every circumstance in any weather even when it rains on them. They embrace the shower cleanse and feel God's tears drenching them while saying thank you for this experience."

-Black Ausar

ASANTE SANA

www.ingramcontent.com/pod-product-compliance
Lightning Source LLC
Chambersburg PA
CBHW072007290426
44109CB00018B/2165